Dreams, Visions and Prophecies 2022

Neha & Evans Francis

notionpress.com

INDIA · SINGAPORE · MALAYSIA

ISBN 979-8-89026-945-4

Contents

Connect with Evans Francis

WhatsApp: https://wa.me/919960877313

YouTube: www.youtube.com/evansfrancis

Facebook: https://www.facebook.com/evansfrancis831

Instagram: https://www.instagram.com/evansfrancis831

Website: www.evansfrancis.org

www.evansfrancisbooks.com

www.christianappdevelopers.com

Email: contact@evansfrancis.org

Join our Telegram Channel: https://t.me/evansfrancis

Introduction

Throughout the Bible, there are numerous instances of men and women of God receiving messages from God, either for themselves or for others. These messages sometimes came through the medium of a vision or a dream or as prophecies, which are inspired utterances, predicting future events, or giving warnings or messages of exhortation.

In this book, Evans shares all the dreams, visions and prophecies that he received from God for the body of Christ in 2021. This book is not the outcome of a day's prayer; it is a product of a continuous walk with the Lord for over a decade and is still in process.

All scripture is given by inspiration of God and is profitable for doctrine, reproof, correction, and instruction in righteousness, that the people of God may be complete, and thoroughly equipped for every good work. And so, we pray this book will be a blessing to you and will give you hope for the future and courage for the present.

God says in Acts 2:17, *"In the last days, I will pour out my Spirit upon all people. Your sons and daughters will prophesy. Your young men will see visions, your old men will dream dreams."* And in Numbers 12:6, He says, *"Now listen to what I say: If there were prophets among you, I, the Lord, would reveal myself in visions. I would speak to them in dreams."*

Dream from The Lord - 1st January 2022

This morning, the Sovereign Lord showed me a dream. In my dream, I saw a well-known pastor sharing the gospel. I was standing at the back, listening to him, when a person came and told me to download his app. I replied that the day I see fruit in his life, I will download it. When he heard what I said, he became angry and frustrated and left the building.

And the Lord said to me, "It is crucial that My children stop following people with gifts but rather follow those who have the fruits of the Spirit. People with gifts can enter into hell, but the people with the fruits will surely live with me."

In His firm grip,

Evans Francis

Vision from The Lord - 9th January 2022

This afternoon as I lay on my bed to rest for a few minutes, the Sovereign Lord showed me a vision. I saw I was standing alone, and Jesus was coming towards me in my vision. I leapt with joy, looking at Him. As He was close to me, one arrow that was supposed to hit me, hit him and pierced into the back of His flesh.

Immediately the Lord said to me, this is how I protect My children who walk with me day and night. So, beloved, walking in the world indeed sounds exciting but walking with God and experiencing His power, provision, and protection is even more exciting.

In His firm grip,

Evans Francis

Prophecy given at House of Deliverance, Nagpur, 9th January 2022

Just as a newborn baby is not given meat to eat, in the same way, I tell you the small details that need to be implemented in your life. If you try to do things before time, that will only harm your life. Remember that the thief's purpose is to steal and kill and destroy. My purpose is to give you a rich and satisfying life. I want you to be victorious in your life. I want you to grow in your life. I want you to be blessed in your life. Just like how a small child depends on his mother for milk, the same way, until and unless you do not grow while depending on Me and remain in Me, you will not be able to see My work in your life.

But remember, just as mother's milk is necessary for the infant, in the same way, My word is necessary for you. If you give the baby anything else instead of milk during his early days, that child may fall ill. In the same way, other than My words, if you give importance to some book or a person or other spirits, then you will never be able to see My work in your life. On the other hand, if you remain in Me, listening to My voice and following My words, you will witness My work in your life, your family, your work, and your business.

Just like in the parable of the Sower and the seed, when the Sower sowed the seeds, some seeds fell on a footpath, others fell on the shallow soil with underlying rock, and some seeds fell among the thorns. In contrast, some other seeds fell on fertile soil, and they produced a crop that was thirty, sixty, and even a hundred times as much as had been planted! If you will help and water My words to work in your life, remember that I will also make you a blessing through your life. But if you become like the shallow or thorny soil, your life will start decreasing instead of increasing.

You can never blame Me for your failures because My Spirit is telling you everything. I am talking to you through My words. Day by day, week by week, you listen to My words and My voice but still, if you won't change, My Spirit will not strive with you always.

Remember the work that I had started with Saul, he could not finish it. Due to his disobedience, I gave his place to David. In the same way, I have no shortage of people. There are many people still sitting in their homes, in My presence, in this city to be anointed by Me so they can go out for My work. If you do not protect your anointing, if you do not protect your calling, and if you do not live your life according to your calling, if you do not change then, you will never be able to see my work in your life.

Just as every child growing up first eats normal soft food, before he can eat everything, in the same way, you are not meant to be a baby throughout your life. As time passes, by listening to My word, you need to mature and grow up. When you walk according to My word, you will grow stronger in life.

Remember King Saul, who was anointed and had My Spirit in him, still, when he saw Goliath of Palestine, he got scared. I did not choose you to be afraid of seeing Goliaths in your life, but be like David who knew that he was anointed, and believed in Me, as he went ahead and faced Goliath and overthrew him. I want the same attitude in your life. The way I trampled Goliath who was a born warrior through David's simple sling, in the same way when you give your simple gift or talent into my hand, I will empower you to destroy the kingdoms of the devil, the works of satan, and break many bondages. I will make you a blessing to many people.

Therefore, in the coming days, if you prepare yourself without forgetting the words that you have heard, and walk according to those words, meditating and thinking about them, while reciting those words, again and again, you will see the seed grow in your life. Just as a mustard plant grows into a great tree, in the same way, the seed sown in your life will become a big tree, that one tree will bless many people, and many people will get shade through it. So, in the coming days, prepare yourself. Without wasting your time, prepare yourself. Walk with Me because the work for which I have chosen you, I want to complete through you, says the Lord God Almighty.

In His firm grip,

Evans Francis

Prophecy given at House of Deliverance, Nagpur, 16ᵗʰ January 2022

Just like a marigold flower that turns where the sun goes, in the same way, I want you to look at Me and move forward according to My will.

Today, many people are walking looking towards the world. Some people are walking looking at their jobs, some are walking looking at their families, some are walking looking at their church, and some are walking looking at sin. But I want you to walk looking at Me because when you walk looking at Me, and the devil brings a bear-like situation before you, you will be able to overcome it. When you walk looking at Me, the devil will bring a lion-like situation in front of you, but you will achieve victory over it. When you walk looking at Me, satan will bring a Goliath-like situation before you, and then you will be able to overcome it and achieve victory over it.

When you walk looking at me, Saul-like situations will come. You will think that I have killed the bear alone, I have killed the lion alone, I have killed Goliath alone, but how will I kill Saul, he has an army, how will I fight? But remember, My word says that in My strength You can crush an army; with Me, you can scale any wall also My word says one person will chase a thousand and two people will chase a ten thousand. When you walk according to Me and follow the path shown by Me, and walk with Me looking at My face like Enoch, according to My will, in fellowship with Me, no matter how great the adversity or situation, I am the God who is enough to give you victory.

Remember, there is a difference between the price of a marigold flower and that of a rose. Marigolds are used for ordinary purposes, but rose flowers are bought only for important things. Hence, its value is more, and it is in your hands whether you want to become a marigold or a rose. It is in your hands whether you do big things or small things in My kingdom. Always remember, I use ordinary people to do extraordinary things. Still, I have a better plan for you, and the devil is working day and night over your life against your family, against your church to destroy that plan, but today, if you are standing, if you are alive, if you can hear My voice, it is because of My grace. You are valuable to Me. Instead of getting lost in the crowd of the world, if you walk with Me the way Enoch walked, I want to be with you, and I want to talk to you. I want to show you My glory as I revealed to the prophet Isaiah, I want to speak to you the way I did with My servant Moses. So, my question to you is this what do you want?

Do you want to have fellowship with me? Do you want to talk with Me? Do you want to see My Glory? Then surrender yourself to Me today itself. If you submit yourself, within the next three months, you will be able to see My glory in your life. Instead of relying upon your wisdom and knowledge, if you obey My Spirit and obey My word, which is settled in Heaven, you will be able to witness My work in your life.

You can't become like Me by living like a worldly person. I took John the Baptist to the wilderness to prepare him. The way I prepare people is different than they think. People think, if they learn from a learned person, they can become a good pastor, a helpful vessel, or a good servant. But the truth is, you can only become a good pastor, helpful vessel, or good servant by walking with Me and by bearing the fruits of My Spirit. That is why you must stop walking behind a pastor, a church, or a denomination. If you walk with Me today, you will be able to see My work in your life, says the Lord God Almighty.

Remember Daniel, he chose to pray rather than become scared looking at the situation. He did not think of the king's decree, he did not think about the consequences of going against the king, which would put him in a situation to be thrown into a lion's den, but he felt it necessary to make fellowship with Me. So, when you make fellowship with Me in your life, then remember that there is no situation that can bring you down, there is no lion whose mouth I cannot shut; similarly, there is no such situation that I cannot change, but you have to go on trusting Me like Daniel. So, it doesn't matter whatever the people say, what the pastor says, what the church says, what the newspaper says, you have to walk with Me, you have to keep on growing with Me.

Remember, those who worked against Daniel were thrown inside the same den of lions in the end. Remember Haman, who prepared the hanging noose for Mordecai and was later hanged by the king on the same snare. So, when you walk with Me, according to My word, when you walk giving Me the first place, then those who stand against you will be thrown into the same pit made by them. The situation that is against you, I can bring down that situation, I am capable of changing that situation, so never consider yourself alone, remember that I am always with you, says the Lord God Almighty.

In His firm grip,

Evans Francis

Dream from The Lord - 21st January 2022

This afternoon as I lay on my bed to rest, the Sovereign Lord showed me a dream. I saw a person who had two snakes and two doves as pets, in my dream. Later he opens them all in one place, and within minutes the snakes attacked the doves and ate them.

And the Lord said to me, this is the current situation of the present Church. They are very active in the things of the devil as well as things of the Holy Spirit, but the things of the devil are overshadowing the things of the Holy Spirit; therefore, My kingdom is suffering a significant loss.

Examine yourself and kill the snakes in your lives so that the doves may live, says the Lord God Almighty.

In His firm grip,

Evans Francis

Message from The Lord - 22ⁿᵈ January 2022

While praying, a message from the Lord came to me saying, "Son, just as a ship and plane take people from one destination to another, and both take a different amount of time to make people reach their destination, both do the same work, but both do it according to their engine, the same way I have chosen you for My work with different capacities and different calling. So, therefore, every person in My kingdom is called for a specific reason to fulfil their destiny in their own time.

Just as a ship cannot sail at the speed of a plane, and a plane cannot fly at the speed of a ship, it is crucial to finish your calling in My time at your pace. It is not important to reach your destination fast, but it is important to reach your destination safely. Unfortunately, many are not able to reach their destination as they try to reach their destination faster rather than safely.

If a plane flies at a ship's speed, it will fall, and the lives of many will perish; the same will happen with the ship if it tries to sail at a plane's speed. It will destroy its engine and people's lives will be in danger. Therefore, if you learn to wait upon Me and run your race in My time, without competing with each other, you will be able to bring many people from darkness to light safely, says the Lord God Almighty."

In His firm grip,

Evans Francis

Prophecy given at House of Deliverance, Nagpur, 23rd January 2022

Nobody likes a donkey. No one uses it for marriages. No king rides on a donkey, but it is only used for the ordinary person for sitting on it or carrying people's belongings. But remember, the Son of God sat on a donkey and came to Jerusalem. Kings and knights ride a horse, never a donkey. If you consider yourself to be like a donkey, unworthy, and think you are of no use, then you are a suitable ride for Me. Through you, I will be able to establish the work of My kingdom.

Today I have many chariots in My body. There are many horses, but I choose things the world considers foolish to shame those who think they are wise and prove to them that I am the living God. So if you listen to My voice, and consider yourself a donkey, remember, as the Son of God rode a donkey, in the same way, He wants to ride your life. He doesn't want to ride your life only when there is a burden or problem, but also in times of joy, in times of sorrow, in times of distress. He wants to ride all the time.

People will despise you, and make fun of you, but the donkey on which Jesus rides is better than a thousand horses. If you dedicate yourself today, Jesus Christ wants to ride on you. The question arises will you allow Christ to ride your life? Do you want to become useful to Jesus?

Many people are locked in their rooms and ready to become a donkey. But, if you dedicate yourself, you will witness the king of glory riding your life. But remember, when Jesus Christ came towards Jerusalem, people shouted, "Hosanna; blessed is the one who comes in the name of the Lord," but later, the same people shouted, "Crucify him." That's why there is no need to choose Me for people because people will change according to time. When people's work is done, they will leave you, but the one who will never leave you, His name is Jesus Christ. He will never leave you or forsake you. He will always be with you whether people like you or not because He loves you, says the Lord God Almighty.

I am about to raise up many John the Baptists in the coming days. This John generation will bring many people back to Me. This generation will share My word without any fear. When John the Baptist spoke against the king and exposed his sinful life, he was murdered. In the same way, in this country, many pastors and servants of God will be murdered but remember they are sowing themselves for Me. The land that sucks their blood, from that land I will raise people in hundreds, thousands, and millions for My name.

The people who are trying to stop My work will never succeed. Till today anyone who has risen up to stop My work has failed. When the church stops fighting in its own strength and comes on its knees to fight the battle, the church will witness My work in this land. Write down what I say, people who are persecuting you today, the same people will preach about Me. I am about to touch people who are persecuting the church. Remember how I made the persecutor Saul change to preacher Paul, in the same way, I am about to touch many Sauls, and in the coming days, you will witness My work.

When the early church underwent persecution, they didn't go to court. They didn't raise up an army to fight. Rather, they came on their knees and prayed. If you walk according to the path, I show you and pray for those who persecute you, those against you will become a part of you. Those who think and speak evil against you will join you. I chose Paul to touch the lives of the gentiles. In the same way, I will use them for My kingdom's expansion; that's why My church must stay awake, and keep praying, says the Lord God Almighty.

In His firm grip,

Evans Francis

Message from The Lord - 28th January 2022

While praying, a message from the Lord came to me saying, son, just as a tree doesn't become a tree within a day, in the same way, a person who comes to Me cannot mature in one day. Just as a tree matures and gives fruit in its time, in the same way, only those who wait upon Me and do as I say will be able to be a helpful vessel for My Kingdom.

Remember, when a tree is in its early stage how a farmer protects it from cows, goats, or animals from consuming it? In the same way, those who believe in Me in the early stage of their walk with Me will be protected from the works of the devil. When a tree becomes huge, no cow, goat or animal can destroy it. In the same way, those who remain in Me and grow with Me will witness a time in their life when no evil plans of people or the devil would be able to harm them. I desire My people to become helpful vessels, says the Lord God Almighty.

In His firm grip,

Evans Francis

Message from The Lord - 10th February 2022

While praying, a message from the Lord came to me saying, son, just like how a small fire can destroy the whole forest, in the same way, the prayers of My children can bring a radical change in their lives, in their city, in their state and their country.

Remember My servant Daniel, who kept on praying for his people even though the devil tried to stop him, in the same way, if My people keep on praying without fear, they will witness My hand in their lives, in their city, in their state and country. The devil has the ability, but you have the authority. The devil was successful in stopping Daniel's prayer for twenty-one days, but as I sent My archangel Michael to help him, in the same way, when My people pray, I will send My angels to fight the principalities of darkness.

In the coming days, India will go through a rough time. There will be no peace in this nation. So, pray for the leaders and all in authority so that you can live peaceful and quiet lives marked by godliness and dignity. Remember, the earnest prayer of a righteous person has great power and produces wonderful results. Stay awake. Keep praying, says the Lord God Almighty.

In His firm grip,

Evans Francis

Message from The Lord - 11ᵗʰ February 2022

While praying, a message from the Lord came to me saying, son, just as a bird builds its nest high or low according to its strength, in the same way, My people need to know their calling, and live their lives as per their calling and anointing.

Just as eagles make their nest in high places, and sparrows build their nests in trees and low areas, keep on doing what I have called you to do. As sparrows, don't try to be like eagles and eagles, don't try to be like sparrows. Do not destroy your calling and anointing by trying to do what you have not been called to do.

Many who didn't live their lives according to their calling and anointing have destroyed their lives, families, ministry, and homes. Therefore, it is important to be faithful in what I have entrusted you with, says the Lord God Almighty.

In His firm grip,

Evans Francis

Message from the Lord - 13th February 2022

This morning, as I lay awake at 2:30, a message from the Lord came to me saying, son, like a female crocodile that carries her newly hatched offspring in her mouth, in the same way I will protect My children - those who believe in My name.

Remember how I cared for and protected the Israelites for forty years in the wilderness? During the day when it was hot, I protected My people with a pillar of cloud and during the night when it was too cold, I protected My people with a pillar of fire. In the same way, I will provide and protect those who walk according to My will.

As a female crocodile stays near her newborn for up to three months, protecting her eggs from predators the same way I wait for My people to grow in Me and I protect them from the snares of the enemies, says the Lord God Almighty.

In His firm grip,

Evans Francis

Prophecy given at House of Deliverance, Nagpur - 13th February 2022

When you look at the grass, it blooms in the night and withers during the day; the same is your life. The time that I have given you, the life that I have given you, live without wasting it.

No one cares about grass, which blooms at night and withers during the day and becomes food for animals. Even though the life span of that grass is for a few hours, the animals live on it. Therefore, you must make your life a blessing for others.

Many plan to do things in the future. Those who rely upon their strength will never be a blessing for others, but the one who will walk according to what I say and do as My word says, that person will be able to be a blessing for others.

Just as a mother takes care of her family, staying in the kitchen from morning to evening, without minding her personal struggles, live your life in the same way without thinking about the struggles in your life.

As Paul poured out himself as an offering to Me, the same way, when you give yourself entirely into My hands, know that through you I can do a wonderful thing in people's lives.

Do not keep things for tomorrow. You plan for that tomorrow that you yourself do not know, but I chose those who live in the present. Those who do My work without wasting any time. Those who spend their life being obedient to My ways. Those who walk in My path without worrying about your future.

Remember, your life is like grass. It's like a bubble that bursts when a small drop of water falls upon it. So, stop playing with your eternity and instead, start living your life seriously with Me, says the Lord God Almighty.

In His firm grip,

Evans Francis

Dream from The Lord - 21ˢᵗ February 2022

This morning the Sovereign Lord showed me a dream. I saw an Australian cricketer die prematurely. His wife was pregnant at that time.

I strongly feel this man has a great calling upon his life, and that's why God is asking us to pray for Him. As you pray for him and his family, pray for your families, relatives, and friends that no premature deaths occur, in Jesus's name.

In His firm grip,

Evans Francis

Message from The Lord - 22nd February 2022

While praying, a message from the Lord came to me saying, son, as a rocket is made and launched with a purpose, in the same way, I have made humans with a plan and purpose. I have chosen My people to reach greater heights in their lives.

Many times, due to human negligence, the rocket is unable to reach its destination and destroys itself on the way. In the same way, My people who do not walk according to My will and My word are unable to reach their destinies due to their negligence.

In the coming days, I desire that, as Elijah repaired the broken altar, My people too must repair the broken areas in their lives. They will reach their destiny and witness My plans and purposes being fulfilled in their lives, says the Lord God Almighty.

In His firm grip,

Evans Francis

Message from The Lord - 23rd February 2022

While praying, a message from the Lord came to me saying, son, as a tree is meant to give shade and bear fruits, in the same way, My people are called to be a blessing to others and bear fruits in their lives. So many are not living according to My will; that's why they are struggling in their lives.

A fish dies when it is taken out of the water. In the same way, those who don't live in the Spirit don't have life. The Spirit alone gives eternal life. Those born of My Spirit will be greatly used for My Kingdom.

As a fish is born, lives and dies in the water, the same way I desire My people to live in the Spirit all the days of their lives and do greater exploits for My Kingdom, says the Lord God Almighty.

In His firm grip,

Evans Francis

Message from The Lord - 24th February 2022

While praying, a message from the Lord came to me saying, son, I desire to raise up many Pauls and Peters for My Kingdom, but they are busy making tents and catching fish. They know they have a call upon their lives but ignore it completely and live for the things of this world.

My Kingdom is suffering due to such people, but I am searching for the violent ones who will take it by force. I am searching for people like those four men who carried a paralyzed man on a sleeping mat. They tried to take him inside but couldn't because of the crowd, they went up to the roof and took off some tiles. Then they lowered the sick man on his mat down into the crowd, right in front of Jesus.

I am searching for people who will go to any extent to save a soul, says the Lord God Almighty.

In His firm grip,

Evans Francis

Prophecy given at House of Deliverance, Nagpur 27ᵗʰ February 2022

As a hunter catches a bird and puts it in a cage for people's amusement, the same way many people's lives and many families have been kept in cages by satan. Many people want to come out of the cage, many people want to fly again, but remember, when the devil catches a person in his cage, he does not leave them easily, but those who believe in Me, when they worship Me day and night and remain in prayer and fasting, I can rescue them like I rescued Peter from prison.

Even though satan has imprisoned you, today you need to know that you do not need to be there forever. Just as I rescued Peter surprisingly, in the same way, I am going to do wonderful things in the life of My children, in many families.

In the coming time, if you don't live and do things to please the world and instead give first place to My work, My word, and Me, you will be able to see My work in your life. Remember, satan always comes to kill, steal and destroy, so when you are in a cage, do not allow satan to do his work.

Remember how Samson repented and how I strengthened him to push the two pillars and destroy the Philistines? In the same way, if you repent and call unto Me, I will give you the strength, power and anointing to break out of that bondage, to break out of satan's cage. It doesn't matter how thick those cage bars or chains might be; I will enable you to break them and use you again for My work.

Once again, you will be able to fly. Once again, you will be able to live for Me. If you surrender yourself to Me, the harm that satan wants to bring in your life, in your family, in your church, I will help you to come such situations. I will fill you with My gifts so that you can come out of it and witness My work in your life.

I want you to fly again. I want you to grow up. I want you to taste the promotions in your life. I have not chosen you to be the tail but the head. So in the coming days, if you surrender yourself, you will see My wonderful work in your life, in your family, in your church, in your ministry, says the Lord God Almighty.

In His firm grip,

Evans Francis

Dream from The Lord - 5th March 2022

This afternoon as I lay on my bed to rest, the Sovereign Lord showed me a dream. First, I saw I was standing on a tall building, and all of a sudden, I saw bathroom pipes bursting. Then, I saw a plumber coming and repairing it.

Within a few minutes, I heard people running here and there, and I saw the sky become black and water as high as a hundred feet coming towards the building. I saw people trying to run away in their cars, but the water came and swept them all away.

All I could understand was that it was an Asian country in my dream. So, therefore, people of God, intercede for your country.

In His firm grip,

Evans Francis

Dream from The Lord - 7th March 2022

This afternoon as I lay on my bed to rest, the Sovereign Lord showed me a dream. I saw one bus standing behind another bus in a signal.

One girl came down from the second bus and tried to cross from the front of the bus. The bus driver didn't see her while she was getting down. As the traffic signal turned green, the bus driver took the bus in front, and this girl was caught between the two buses. Immediately she bent down, but her hand got jammed between the two buses, but nothing happened to her life.

And the Lord said to me, today many believers who are going through trials in their lives would have been crushed by the devil, but it is My grace they are still alive. So, therefore, they must become serious about their lives and live for My kingdom.

In His firm grip,

Evans Francis

Dream from The Lord - 9ᵗʰ March 2022

This morning the Sovereign Lord showed me a dream. In my dream, I saw Moderna COVID-19 Vaccine being sold in India in very large quantities. Therefore, the people of God must pray that there should be no rise in Covid-19 cases in India.

In His firm grip,

Evans Francis

Prophecy given at House of Deliverance, Nagpur 6th March 2022

Relying on their own strength, Moses' parents managed to hide him for some time, but when he was growing up, due to his crying, they could not keep him in their house Defeated, they left Moses in the Nile River.

Today many of My people are living their life depending on their own understanding, and because of that, they are stuck in many situations. But the way Moses' mother believed in Me and handed over her "Moses situation" into My hand, in the same way, if today you give yourself into My hands, without relying upon your understanding and wisdom, if you surrender yourself completely in My hands, then you will be able to witness My work in your life, in your family, in your church, and your ministry.

Remember when Moses' mother handed Moses into My hands, and I brought him into Pharoah's palace? In the same way, if you put yourself, your talents, your gifts, your life, your family, your ministry, and your church into My hands, then I am the God who can take it where it is supposed to be.

Do not rely upon your own understanding and wisdom, My son and My daughter, you will not be successful in your work for long, but remember that when Moses' mother handed over Moses to me, I taught him and made him a knight, and due to that you can read five books of the Bible because a mother gave her son in My hand. When you give your talents, your gifts to Me, know that I am the God capable of making it a blessing to millions of people. Do not consider yourself alone or poor. Gold and silver belong to Me. Heaven is my throne, and the earth is my footstool. That's why you must keep on moving forward having faith in Me.

Many of you are like a bird whose wings have been destroyed by a hunter. You want to fly, but you cannot fly. You are sitting in front of me today with such wounds, but remember what My word says, those who believe in Me will chase a thousand, and two people put ten thousand to flight.

I will fill you with My power, My anointing, and My gifts so that you can fly again. You can once again do the work for which I have chosen you. Satan wants to keep you seated, but remember I chose you not to sit but to fly. I chose you to run, not to fall. I have not chosen you to be the tail but to make you the head. No shadow of shame will darken your faces, says the Lord God Almighty.

In His firm grip,

Evans Francis

Dream from The Lord - 16th March 2022

This morning the Sovereign Lord showed me a dream. In my dream, I saw that Vodafone's mobile phone service had stopped completely, and millions of people were troubled due to it. So, if God showed me this, He wants us to pray for it. 1 John 5:14-15: "And we are confident that he hears us whenever we ask for anything that pleases him. And since we know he hears us when we make our requests, we also know that he will give us what we ask for."

In His firm grip,

Evans Francis

Dream from The Lord - 25th March 2022

This morning, the Sovereign Lord showed me a dream. In my dream, I saw people eating rice mixed with their urine. And the Lord said to me, as unhygienic as it looks, in the same way, My people are living in sin and leading an unholy life. Therefore, it is time My people turn from every type of sinful activity and live a holy life.

In His firm grip,

Evans Francis

Prophecy given at House of Deliverance, Nagpur 27th March 2022

As I reminded Pharoah's chief cupbearer about Joseph, in the same way, many people who had forgotten you will remember you in the coming days. Those who achieved things in their life because of you and have forgotten you will remember you.

Some people are going to search for you and find you. Some people will get your number from other people. Some people are going to send friends requests to connect with you. Remember, man can forget what you have done, but I remember everything.

Due to Joseph's ministry, the cupbearer was back in the palace. Many homes that would have been broken are standing strong due to your prayers and fasting. Those who didn't have a job got the job. People's lives were on the verge of destruction, but I restored them through your prayers. Many such people have forgotten you. Those who have tasted your ministry and were blessed will remember you back. Those who have been blessed by your life and threw you away are coming back.

People who spoke against you, people who mocked you, those who tried to assassinate your character, I will use the same people to elevate you. The same people will celebrate you. Such people, I will use you to reach your destination. I was preparing Joseph to become the governor of the whole of Egypt. In the same way, I am preparing you. So stop grieving for people who were blessed by your ministry, life, and prayers; rather, remember that all glory goes to My name alone.

When I work, only I receive the glory. I am never too late, never too early, I am right on time. I am the God who works at the right time. I am the God who sends My blessings at the right time. I am the God who answers prayers at the right time. I am the God who heals at the right time. I am the God who delivers at the right time. I am the God who restores broken houses at the right time.

In the coming days, humble yourselves and spend more time in My presence; then you will witness My work in your life, your family, and your ministry. This is not the time to grieve. This is not the time to mourn. Because I am the God who turns mourning into dancing, says the Lord God Almighty.

In His firm grip,

Evans Francis

Prophecy given at House of Deliverance, Nagpur - 3rd April 2022

Just as a lion sits in hiding so that he catches an animal and destroys it, satan is waiting to steal the blessings I have given you, steal the peace that I have given you, and steal the gifts I have given you. He will try his level best to destroy it and make it useless. So, in the coming days, you need to protect the talents, gifts, blessings and anointing that I have given you.

The gifts, blessings and the anointing that I have given you, if you do not keep it safe, just as the Philistines destroyed Samson's life with the help of Delilah, the same way satan will ruin your life by bringing the wrong people in your life. So be careful in the days to come, with whom you spend time, with whom you sit, with whom you talk, and with whom you share your secrets. If you do not protect your gift, if you do not save your anointing, the same condition that happened to Samson will happen to your life.

The work I wanted to get done through Samson, he could do only a part of it because he did not follow the path shown by Me. Yet when he repented before Me, I heard his weeping and crying and anointed him again so that he might destroy many Philistines in his death. Samson repented, and I forgave his mistakes by not remembering his past and again filled him with My power. In the same way, if you surrender yourselves into My hands without remembering your past, then you will witness My work in your life, in your family, in your ministry, and in your business.

Today my church is sleeping with its head on Delilah's lap. So many kinds of Delilahs the devil has brought into My children's lives. Where Samson was supposed to fight and work for Me, he enjoyed lying down on the lap of Delilah, and when he despised Me and followed his carnal lust, the devil stole the power, the anointing on his life.

It's time to destroy the Delilah of your life. Every person who separates you from Me, everything and anything that separates you from sitting in prayer is a Delilah in your life. My Spirit will not always strive with you. So, this is the time to surrender, repent, and follow Me. If you walk alone, a lion is waiting for you to be alone. He will come and tear you apart and destroy you. So stay alert, stay awake, stay in the faith, keep on praying, don't despise the gifts of the Holy Spirit, and live in Me, says the Lord God Almighty.

In His firm grip,

Evans Francis

Prophecy given at House of Deliverance during Good Friday Service, Nagpur 15th April 2022

Just as a flower is meant to remain in a plant, I have chosen you to remain in Me. When people like a flower, they cut that flower and keep it in water. Because of the beauty of the flower, they remove it from the plant – the original source of its life and keep it in water - an artificial environment. That flower stays in the water for a few days, but it withers.

Similarly, I have chosen you to remain in Me., Seeing your beauty, seeing your anointing, seeing your talent, many people will try to separate you from Me. When they separate you, they will not plant you in the soil because they know that if you stay in the soil, you will sprout again. That's why they will keep you in artificial water instead of soil.

In the beginning, you will blossom when you walk and live with them. Your flowers will not wither, but a time will come when you will start withering, and there will come a time when you will dry and die. That's what the devil wants.

I want you to bear long-lasting fruit, but Satan will bring the wrong people into your life and will not allow the fruit to grow. Before that time, he will try to take you away from Me and keep you in an artificial environment and grow you in falsehood, in the wrong things, in false hope, in the false promises and eventually destroy you. You can never fulfil the purpose I have chosen unless you remain in Me.

Three things will happen if you remain in Me. First, you will bear fruit. Second, you will be able to see the answers to your prayers, and third, you will be able to enter into My eternal life. These three things can only happen if you remain in Me. When you live in an artificial environment, your life might bear fruit for a season, but it will be destroyed eventually, and you will never be able to see the answers to your prayers and never enter into eternal life.

So, in the days to come, in the times to come, you need to examine yourself and see if you are in Christ or not. Do you desire the applause of the people than the anointing I have poured over your life? " Examine yourself. If you did not consider it right to live for Christ, are you separated from Him, and have you started living in an artificial environment?

Where do you find yourself? Today is the time to come back. The soil is still soft. I can bring forth more fruits through you. I can use you more. I can make you a ray of hope for many. I have only one question, do you want it?

In His firm grip,

Evans Francis

Dream from The Lord – 28th April 2022

Today afternoon while I lay to rest for a few minutes, the Sovereign Lord showed me a dream. I saw a house where two boys, one aged four and another aged one, came out of nowhere. These kids had no one. So instead of being taken care of at home, they were sent to the police to send them to some orphanage. These kids were not looking good at all.

And the Lord said to me, these two kids represent souls that do not belong to good families, and the house represents the Church. I have been sending souls to many churches, but they ignore them, and ultimately satan destroys My plans in their lives. A Church that looks at colour, clothes and finance can never be a house of Mine but rather a place of satan says the Lord God Almighty.

In His firm grip,

Evans Francis

Dream from The Lord - 10ᵗʰ May 2022

This morning the Sovereign Lord showed me a dream. In my dream, I saw some people on top of a hill and they were shooting arrows at all the houses beneath. When I opened the door, the arrows were coming straight towards me. However, I was able to dodge the arrows without injuring myself. Then, I saw a small baby around one year old taking an arrow which was lying on the floor and going inside.

As I saw it, I immediately asked the family to throw that arrow away as it was a planned attack, but they ignored me. As I asked them to inform the police, those throwing the arrows were trying to intimidate me, but I wasn't scared. The following day when we woke up, everybody's door locks were broken, and I saw my neighbour purchase a heavy lock for protection.

And the Lord said to me, this is what is happening in the body of Christ. The enemy is constantly throwing wrong teaching at My people— those who are babes in Christ accepting the false gospel and taking it inside their homes. So again, the Lord said to me, do not be intimidated by the enemy; keep on warning My people as I have appointed you as a watchman over My people. Tell My people, it's not the lock but My word that protects them against such false teachings.

In His firm grip,

Evans Francis

Prophecy given at House of Deliverance, Nagpur 8ᵗʰ May 2022

When you look at a duck above the water, it looks beautiful and calm in appearance, but its feet keep moving underwater so that it can stay above the water. In the same way, when you see people who have a perfect life, their lives are happy, there is peace in their lives, there is love in their lives, their family and their children are growing in Me, and they are witnessing My blessings in their lives. But what you don't see is, to maintain those blessings, to maintain that happiness, to maintain that love, that peace, they keep fighting sin and evil every day.

If you want to see My blessings in your life, if you want to see My growth in your life, if you want to feel and see My love, My protection, My peace in your life, then every day you need to wrestle, not with your brothers and sister, not with the people of the church, but with the forces of darkness and the devil who wants to steal the blessings of your life, who wants to bring death into your life, who wants to bring infertility into your life. He who fights will be able to see My work in his life.

Remember, you are not fighting against flesh-and-blood enemies, but against evil rulers and authorities of the unseen world, against mighty powers in this dark world, and evil spirits in the heavenly places. That's why, instead of fighting with human beings, it is important to destroy the devil who attacks in secret. Do not allow the devil to work in your life rather, lead a holy life. When you live a holy life in Me, then you will see all My blessings in your life. You will see My growth in your life, family, business, and work.

But if you try to sail on two boats, you will fall flat on your face and fail. So, therefore, do not just look at people who are growing in Me rather, understand that secret and apply that secret in your life and when you walk, you will be able to see My work in your life, in your family, in your church, and every one of your situations, says the Lord God Almighty.

In His firm grip,

Evans Francis

Dream from The Lord - 20th May 2022

This afternoon, while I was resting, the Sovereign Lord showed me a dream. I saw a well-secured house, and a snake entering it. It was huge, black and venomous. One person in the family said, Years ago, a snake entered our house, but it was killed. How come this new snake has now entered our home?"

And the Lord God Almighty said to me, "I had delivered many houses from the snares of the devil, but sadly, by their own wrong decisions, the devil has entered their lives again. Therefore, if My people will not repent for their sinful actions and turn from their wicked ways, the devil will work devastatingly."

In His firm grip,

Evans Francis

Prophecy given at House of Deliverance, Nagpur 15th May 2022

Just as a person separates raw rice and throws away the dirt from it, in the same way, I am going to clean My church. This is because so many unwanted people [goats] have come into My church and defy My name instead of glorifying it. I will separate such persons and families from My church so that my church will be flawless, holy and wrinkle-free in the coming days, for which, Jesus himself will return.

As long as there is sin and filth in the church, it cannot be holy and cannot fulfil the task for which I have established My church. I am not only talking about this church, but I am talking about the whole worldwide church. My church is doing everything except for the very thing I have chosen to do. Today in the church, only the world can be seen, not Me. Today in the church, there is no purity, it is filled with filthiness and sin. I want My church to be ready to accomplish the task I have chosen for it.

Suppose a person eats rice mixed with pebbles and dirt, he will soon fall ill. In the same way, when a church is united with the world, there is sin. So those who come to Me through that church will be sick and weak and when the storm comes into their lives, they will not be able to face it because the church has not been able to teach them the truth. So in the coming days, there is a need to examine your life without wasting any time.

You need to test your church and your ministry, hold on to what is good, throw away the bad, separate it from your lives, and walk in holiness. I am with you. I will finish the work I have started with you. Do not give a chance to satan and to wrong associations to work in your life. Keep on walking with Me in holiness and be faithful in the work I have given to you, says the Lord God Almighty.

In His firm grip,

Evans Francis

Visions & Prophecy given at House of Deliverance, Nagpur 29th May 2022

1st Vision

While we were singing a song, God showed me a vision. In that vision, I saw there was a swampy land, and when people started singing, an asphalt road rose out of that swamp.

Many of you are going through a situation where you find yourself in the swamp, but God will make a way for you that is quite impossible for men. It is not easy to make a road in the midst of a swamp. In the same way, in every impossible situation that you are going through, God is going to surprise you.

2nd Vision

As we continued to worship, God showed me another vision. In this vision, I saw there was a cage, and in that cage, there was a bird, and this bird thought that it was going to live in this cage for life. But suddenly a hand came, and opened the door of the cage, and the bird was set free.

Many of you are in a caged situation where you might think you will never be free, but God is about to do something so beautiful that you will be free from every caged situation.

Prophecy

Just as Satan tried many times to destroy My servant, David, first by a lion, then by a bear, then by Goliath, and then by King Saul. But they all failed. In the same way, no tricks of satan will prevail in your life as long as you keep My anointing in your life.

David was not perfect, but he did not hold back in accepting his mistakes. Whenever I showed him his error, he became humble, acknowledged his mistake, and completed the task for which I chose him. He was able to finish the race which he started. I want you to finish your race. I want you to fulfil your calling. The work for which I have chosen you is not a tiny task. Many people are sitting in front of me to do that work, but among them, I have chosen you for my work. Will you give your life to me today? I want to do significant work through you. A task that you have never thought of because my thinking is beyond your thinking. You deserve more than what you desire; I didn't give you what you want because your desire is small.

Live your life looking at me, and you will understand what you are worth. Stop judging your life through the eyes of the world. Stop living by the standards of the world. Stop being like the world. Live a holy life because I am holy. Live a spiritual life because I am Spirit. When David worshipped alone, he did not have an audience, he did not have a stage, but he used to worship me alone in front of me. Everyone could see King Saul wherever he stood because he was the tallest. Man's eyes went to Saul, but My eyes went to David, whom no one could see. Stop underestimating yourself because I am your God, the creator of the heavens and the earth, and heaven is My throne and earth is My footstool. The day you understand who you are in Me, you will understand who I am. When you start living in Me, you will start to understand yourself better.

No one saw David, but My eyes saw him. He was alone and had no one, and there was no parent's love, no brothers' support, and no family, but I became his shepherd because he allowed Me in his life. So if you dedicate yourself to Me today, I have made a big plan for you. You are not ordinary; you are extraordinary in Me, says the Lord God Almighty.

In His firm grip,

Evans Francis

Visions & Prophecy given at House of Deliverance, Nagpur 5th June 2022

1st Vision

While we were worshipping, the Sovereign God showed me a vision. I saw a person walking down the road, and a mountain came before him. The person was going through a crooked and narrow path. So, when this person looked towards the mountain, he saw a hand coming from the sky and pressing that mountain down. The mountain became flat, and that person continued his journey.

Many of you are going through a narrow way [the right way] in your life, but out of nowhere many mountains have come up in front of you and you don't know what to do. Do not be discouraged. You are about to witness the hand of God work supernaturally in your life. Impossible mountains will be turned into beautiful valleys in Jesus' name.

2nd Vision

While we were worshipping, the Sovereign Lord showed me another vision. It was indeed a beautiful vision. God showed me a newborn baby. A boy who was just born. He was very beautiful to look at. God told me just as a mother gives birth after carrying her child for nine months, in the same way, many people have been praying for many things for many months. Finally, they are about to witness an answer to their prayers in the coming days.

Remember, beloved, a delay is not denial. God's timing is perfect. Do not lose hope. The best is yet to come in Jesus' name.

3ʳᵈ Vision

I saw another vision: angels coming down from heaven in a line, with a sword in their hands. God is working wonderfully in your lives.

God is sending His angels to work on your behalf. So do not be worried or dismayed. He will do a wonderful thing in your life, in Jesus' name.

Prophecy

Just as Solomon did not keep his heart under control and married many women who took him to other gods and away from Me, satan is bringing the wrong people into many people's lives. As I did not allow Samson to perish, in the same way, I have shown them My grace and helped them come out of bad relationships.

In the coming days, I will do such a thing that when people see that work, they will say that God's justice has descended on this family. People will say that God's judgment has fallen on this church. People will say that God's justice has dropped on this pastor's life because now the time has come where My kingdom has to grow, and I am going to raise many youngsters for the growth of My kingdom. Young men who will be filled with My Spirit, in the knowledge of My word, who will be filled with the gifts of My Spirit and will do My work with signs and wonders.

The time to come will be lamentable, difficult, and painful, but in the midst of all this, I will take care of My children in a beautiful way, like how I fed My children with manna and gave them water in the desert. Those who are mine will not see any deficiency. They will experience My blessings in their life and will be a blessing to many.

Therefore, in the coming days, you need to spend time in My presence. When the bridegroom comes, those who stay awake will go to be with the bridegroom, and the believers who are sleeping, those who are not ready, will be left behind, so make good use of the time I have given you and move forward, says the Lord God Almighty.

In His firm grip,

Evans Francis

Visions given at House of Deliverance, Nagpur 12th June 2022

1st vision

While we were singing, the Spirit of God showed me a vision. In the vision, I saw the husk of a pea, and God said that the husk is meant to protect the peas so that they can be useful. We eat it as a vegetable and sow it as a seed so that it can grow. Still, sometimes we open a pod and find a small hole in them. Through this hole, the worm enters the pod and starts eating the peas one by one and the worm gets bigger.

Beloved, when you give the devil a chance, he will never hesitate to come into your life to destroy it. Stay alert. Stay safe in Christ Jesus.

2nd vision

As we continued to worship, God showed me another vision. Again, the Spirit of God said that as the sun rises and sets and everybody can see these things, in the same way, God is going to do a great thing in your life that people can see. Something that you did not imagine. When the sun rises and sets, millions and billions of people see it. In the same way, many people will see the great thing God is about to do in your life and will be amazed to see what has happened.

3rd Vision

When we were singing, the Spirit of God reminded me of the miracle when Jesus Christ raised Lazarus from the dead, after being kept for four days in the tomb. And when he came out of the grave, Jesus Christ said, "Untie him." While you are singing this song, the Spirit of God has shown that there are ropes that you have been tied with, with the intention that this person should never grow up, that this person should never prosper in his life, this person should never get a promotion and never receive and earn any respect in his life. In this way, satan has tied many people with ropes. But when you sing this song, those ropes are burning and breaking, and God is working wonderfully in your life. So, rejoice. God is about to do a wonderful thing in your life.

4ᵗʰ Vision

When Stephen was being taken out of the city and stoned with false accusations, he saw heaven open and Jesus Christ sitting at the right hand of God. Stephen didn't compromise. He told the truth even though people didn't like it. Those people became furious, dragged him out, and stoned him to death. Those who stoned him to death didn't see that vision, but Stephen, who was going through pain, saw that beautiful vision.

In the coming days, whatever situation might come, let us make a covenant with God that we will not compromise. "I will do what your word says and not do what it doesn't say. I will not turn left or right from your word. I will live for you. I will live for you."

In His firm grip,

Evans Francis

Dream from The Lord - 19th June 2022

This morning the Sovereign Lord showed me a dream. In my dream, I saw a lady school principal in my city molesting two boys from her school. One boy was around fifteen years old, while the other was twelve or thirteen. Both the boys were scared but couldn't do anything. She was using them sexually.

The Sovereign Lord said, "If she doesn't repent and turn from her wicked ways, she and her school will experience God's wrath." I don't want to mention the name. I just want this post to reach her and hope she repents and turns from her wicked ways.

In His firm grip,

Evans Francis

Dream from The Lord - 22nd June 2022

This morning the Sovereign Lord showed me a dream. In my dream, I saw a large ground, and on that ground, I saw all the religious places of worship in one place, including a Church. I saw those going to Church entering the mosque, those entering the mosque entering temples, and those entering the temples entering gurudwara, etc. I saw so many worship places that I didn't even know about.

And the Lord said, soon a time is coming when My people will lose faith in Me and start believing all ways lead to Me. There will arise a great deception and will deceive the elect. One world religion is on its way. People of God, prepare yourself. Your bridegroom is coming soon.

In His firm grip,

Evans Francis

Dream from The Lord - 26th June 2022

This morning the Sovereign Lord showed me a dream. In my dream, I saw a lady who was very lean in stature whose bones I could see, but she was gifted to teach the children and pray ferociously.

And the Lord said to me, many people are gifted within the body of Christ, but the Church has failed to take care of them, and My kingdom is suffering due to it. My people are governed by committees - men who are carnal in their minds and are not led by My Spirit. Therefore, the body of Christ, repair your altars and get right with God.

In His firm grip,

Evans Francis

Dream from The Lord - 27th June 2022

This morning the Sovereign Lord showed me a dream. In my dream, I saw a cage. In that cage, I saw four birds. Three birds were jungle babblers, and one was a sparrow. In the beginning, everything seemed fine. But slowly, the jungle babblers started to attack that sparrow. Soon after, the attack became ferocious, and they killed the sparrow.

And the Lord said to me, this is what is happening within the Church. Juggle babbler represents the old believers and the sparrow the new believer. When a new believer comes, the church people accept them gladly, but slowly, as they come to know their weaknesses, they attack them and sometimes even kill them spiritually and destroy their faith.

Beware, people of God, that you don't turn out to be jungle babblers.

In His firm grip,

Evans Francis

Dream from The Lord – 2nd July 2022

This morning, the Sovereign Lord showed me a dream. In my dream, I saw I was waiting to catch a bus, and a young man came and asked for directions to a hospital address. I didn't know, so I asked him to check with the autorickshaw driver, and he guided him properly. As he was leaving, I asked him what had happened. He said somebody shot my dad, and he is in the hospital. I replied I would visit him.

The next moment I saw I was at the gate of a huge church—a massive building. I went inside and started telling them about this young man and asked them to accompany me to the hospital, so we could pray. Surprisingly nobody seemed interested. One person said we have so many courses, men and women, and youth groups, and they were not interested in winning a soul.

And the Lord told me this is what is happening within the Church. They are running programmes instead of winning souls. People of God, winning souls should be the priority of every believer. A church that is not focused on winning souls is losing.

In His firm grip,

Evans Francis

Dream from The Lord - 2nd July 2022

In my second dream, I saw two trucks moving simultaneously on the same road. There was no space for another one, yet a truck bashed them from the back, and all three trucks collided, and a big accident occurred.

Surprisingly many were injured, but only a few died. I saw one person's head lying separately on the ground. There were women and children on the ground.

People of God, pray that no such accident occurs and no one should die without knowing our Lord and Saviour Jesus Christ.

In His firm grip,

Evans Francis

Dream from The Lord - 9th July 2022

This afternoon, while I was resting, the Sovereign Lord showed me a dream. I saw I was telling a person that I am travelling to Indonesia for ministry, and this person said it was a waste of time to travel so far. "You just do one thing, send some money that's enough," he said. I replied, "Hasn't Jesus told us to go around all the world and preach the gospel?"

And the Lord told me, "This is the thinking of present-day believers. Giving money has taken the place of witnessing and sharing the gospel. The church will never grow until and unless it shares the gospel of Jesus Christ."

In my second dream, I saw an African preacher. He was carrying his photo in his hand and was asking people, "Do you know me? Do you recognize me?" When people couldn't, he would become sad and grieve. This was happening over and over again.

And the Lord said to me that these are modern-day preachers who want to be known in this world, not in the future. They want a name and fame for themselves. Beloved, it doesn't matter how many people know you. Ask yourself a question, does Jesus knows you? That matters the most.

In His firm grip,

Evans Francis

Visions & Prophecy given at House of Deliverance, Nagpur 19th June 2022

Vision

While singing this song, the Spirit of God showed a vision. An old man was walking with a staff. I didn't see his face. Then I saw that Jesus Christ walked behind him, put His hand on the older man's shoulder, and started walking with him.

Maybe any of you here or those who watch us on YouTube and Facebook, have a concern in your mind that 'When I am old, who will take care of me? When I am old then my son or daughter, will they take care of me or not, or will they leave me alone?'

Beloved, I am not an old man by experience, but one thing I want to say is that never trust any human being, and do not put your hope on your children, put your hope on the Lord Jesus, He will guide you, He will come and carry you forward, cast your burdens on Him and move forward.

He knows the future. Commit your future into His hands. Don't spoil your present by thinking about the future. The time God has given you, live happily with your children when they are with you, and have faith in God. As the song goes, in my weakness. When we're old, we'll be weak. Time will come when we'll be in need of a walker, but as the song says, in my weakness, no man will help rather, only Lord Jesus Christ will be our strength. Amen!

Prophecy

When you go out, you wear sandals or shoes so that your feet do not get soiled, but those sandals and shoes save you from getting dust on your feet and from thorns and broken glass pieces. They protect you from injuring your feet or getting injured. Similarly, I have placed My servants, the Church and the Word of God in your life to save your soul, so that whatever hurt or injury can happen to you, it's their responsibility to make you aware of that and to prepare you beforehand. So when My Spirit speaks to you, do not despise it, rather consider it important and implement that in your life.

In the coming days, various Pastors from different Churches will send spies to your Church, saying that you go and see what happens over there that does not happen here. But remember, whoever acts in such a wrong way like this in My Kingdom, I'll bring punishment in their lives, families, and ministries. If any person plays with My Word and My Spirit, he'll surely be punished by Me.

So, in the coming days, keep yourself safe and stand firm on My Word, without wasting your time, as you continue doing the work for which I have chosen you. You will be able to see My work in your life.

Don't think that I don't have wisdom, understanding and knowledge. When King Solomon asked Me for wisdom and knowledge, I gave it to him, then why won't I give it to you? Don't think that you are alone. Don't underestimate yourself because the work for which I sent you is not a small task, rather I have planted you in this Church according to My great plan. And in the coming days, months and years, you will see My work in your life.

Anyone who will run before My time will not see My work, but he who believes in Me and prioritizes Me and My work will witness Me working in his life, family, and ministry.

I have chosen many people to come here, but the devil is stopping them from coming. So, there is a need to pray for those sheep in the coming days so that those sheep can reach here safely. And no wolf, animal, or devil can destroy them or their soul.

I am always with you. Therefore, do not consider yourself alone. I will never leave you nor forsake you, says the Lord God Almighty.

In His firm grip

Evans Francis

Vision from The Lord - 19th July 2022

While I was about to sleep, the Sovereign Lord showed me a vision. I saw a place where there were about 40-50 beds. All the people there were injured. Then, suddenly, a mob came in and burnt them all. So, I sensed that one religious group was taking revenge upon another.

People of God, pray that no communal riots take place in India. Pray harder.

In His firm grip,

Evans Francis

Dream from The Lord - 22nd July 2022

This morning the Sovereign Lord showed me a dream. In my dream, I saw an Indian person standing on a terrace, and a US fighter came in front of him and fired a missile. This person jumped from his terrace, and simultaneously the rocket hit his house, and all his family members died in it. I could feel the emptiness and pain of that person and the feeling of becoming an orphan.

And the Lord told me, there is a devil's plan to destroy the relationship between India and USA. So, people of God, rise up, stand in the gap, and intercede for your nation.

In His firm grip,

Evans Francis

Dream from The Lord - 27th July 2022

This morning the Sovereign Lord showed me a dream. In my dream, I saw a man standing in the backyard of his house. All of a sudden, three huge tigers came out of nowhere. This man had the chance to run inside and close the door, but on the contrary, some bricks were lying there. He decided to pick them up and threw them at the tigers. Soon enough, the bricks were over, and the tigers attacked him. As I ran to save him, a dog came out of nowhere and ran ahead of me. When I reached the place, I thought the man had died, but he was severely injured but alive, and the dog had killed all three tigers.

And the Lord said to me, this is the present-day church. Instead of protecting itself, the church likes to play with satan and then get defeated. It's the grace of God that He sends His angels to protect them. A beaten and badly injured church can be witnessed in today's world.

In His firm grip,

Evans Francis

Message from The Lord - 4th August 2022

While praying, a message from the Lord came to me saying, "Son, when I asked Ananias to go to Saul and lay hands on him so he can see, in the same way, I am raising an "Ananias Generation" that will not seek fame, those who will be obedient to what I say and lastly those who won't be judgemental - those who will not look at the outer appearance.

I am raising up a generation whom I will tell what to do, what to say and where to go. A generation that can go through anything for My name. A generation that is okay to be unknown in this world but their names will be greatly known in My kingdom.

My church must pray for this "Ananias Generation" so these chosen youngsters will stand for My name without any fear, without any double thoughts and will not love their lives but rather be faithful to Me and finish what I have chosen for.

In His firm grip,

Evans Francis

Prophecy given at House of Deliverance, Nagpur 7th August 2022

Just as I saw Hannah's tears, I saw your tears. Just like Peninnah used to make fun of Hannah by looking at the barrenness in her life, likewise, there are people in your life who like to make fun of you by looking at the shortcomings/ weaknesses in your life. But the way I worked in Hannah's life, the same way I will work in your life too.

Eli, being a priest himself, could not understand Hannah's cry. When you are sitting in My presence today, you've told your problems to many men of God, but they did not give importance to your moaning nor took it seriously. You've shared your situation with many people, but they also could not understand you.

You've shared with your family, parents, and siblings, but they too could not understand you. But God says I know your situation, your groaning, your loneliness. So when you cry alone on the terrace, while driving your vehicle, you're crying so that no one can see you, because if they see you crying, they will make fun of you and ask you what did this God give you?

But just as I turned Hannah's lament into dancing, in the days to come, I will do a wonderful thing in your life, family, ministry, and church.

The coming days are not for weeping but of joy, not of lamenting but of dancing. That's why the time has come to remember My works. Like how Miriam worshipped with a tambourine, worship Me all the time. When you worship Me continually, you will see a significant change in your situation.

The people who rejected you, and those who ridiculed you, will come searching for you. I will prepare a table for you in front of your enemies, in front of those who mock you, who make fun of you, and who make you cry, says the Lord God Almighty.

In His firm grip,

Evans Francis

Prophecy given at House of Deliverance, Nagpur 21ˢᵗ August 2022 By Evans Francis

Just as my twelve disciples turned this earth upside down, in the same way, I want to use everyone in this Church for My work. But as long as My people whom I call, won't prepare themselves, then no matter how much I wish, they would not see My work in their lives.

Shadrach, Meshach, and Abednego saw Me in the fire as they were ready to go through it. Daniel saw me in the lion's den as he was prepared to go into the den. Abraham saw the work of My hand on one of the Mountains in Moriah as he was ready to sacrifice his son. Noah could see My hand, and because of his faith, his family got saved as he listened to My voice and obeyed Me.

On the contrary, when Lot went to Sodom, he left My fellowship. There he couldn't even find God-fearing sons-in-law for his daughters. But Noah was able to choose good wives for his sons. So, when you walk in My ways, then only you will be able to see My work in your life.

Many people ask Me why I am not using you the way I used Peter and Paul. So many people don't see My work because they don't understand their calling. John the Baptist never did any miracle, but there was no one like him.

So don't go after miracles. When you go after winning the souls, when you become a seeker of My Kingdom, then I will give everything to you. You will be able to see spiritual gifts and blessings in your life, but if you go after the spiritual gifts, if you do as Simon tried, to buy spiritual gifts, then you will never see My work in your life.

If you go after the comfort and blessings of the world, you will never be able to enter My Kingdom. So, it is necessary to continue your walk while seeking My Kingdom and understanding your calling.

I am always with you, says the Lord God Almighty.

In His firm grip,

Evans Francis

Vision from The Lord – 25th August 2022

While praying, the Sovereign Lord showed me a vision. In my vision, I saw a massive train accident taking place. People of God, pray that no such incident takes place. No premature deaths in Jesus' name.

In His firm grip,

Evans Francis

Prophecy given at House of Deliverance, Nagpur 4ᵗʰ September 2022

Just as a fish is made to live inside the water and an animal is made to live on land, I have created you to be with me. If a fish is taken out of the water, it will live for some time but it will die. In the same way, if an animal goes into the water, it will also die in a while but both the fish and the animal will suffer before dying because both were trying to live in a situation for which they were not created.

I created man to have fellowship with Me, but death came into man's life because of sin. A fish and an animal have no hope after death, but you have hope. I hope that you can have the fellowship that I wanted from Adam and Eve with Me. To have that fellowship, you must remain in Me till you die on this earth.

Many people are living in artificial fellowship. Just as a premature baby, born before birth, is kept in an incubator, My people are spending their lives in different incubators without being with Me. That is why they cannot see My work in their life. They are trying to achieve something with their own strength. The person who tries to achieve something on their own strength will never succeed in their work because, as My word says, not by might nor by power, but by My Spirit. When you live your family life through My Spirit, when you do your ministry through My Spirit and live your life through My Spirit, then only you will see My wonderful work in every area of your life.

I am still the same God as when Isaac sowed in the famine and reaped hundred times. There is no circumstance in which I cannot work. There is no problem for which I do not have a solution. There is no pain for which I have no cure. There are no tears that I cannot wipe. There is no disease that I cannot cure because the keys to life and death are in My hands. He who believes in Me will have eternal life, but he who does not believe has already condemned himself.

It's time to examine yourself. It's time to return to Me just like the prodigal son, who returned to his father after realising his mistake. Just as his father waited for his son, I am also waiting for you in the same way. I only have one question: will you listen to My call? Will you listen to My voice? Will you accept or reject My invitation? Remember the decision you take in your life today will be echoed in eternity.

Don't waste your time because a dark night is coming, a night when Christians' lives will be tough. A night where My work will be negligible, but when that time comes, understand that My coming is near, so stay awake, be alert, keep praying, do not extinguish the Spirit, do not despise prophecy, says the Lord God Almighty.

In His firm grip,

Evans Francis

Prophecy given at House of Deliverance, Nagpur 4ᵗʰ September 2022

Just as good and bad tomatoes are kept in the same basket to be sold, you are in this world too. When people come to buy, they select good tomatoes; only rotten ones are left in the basket. The shopkeeper tries to sell that rotten tomato at a low price, and some people purchase it.

There were many good tomatoes [people] that I had chosen for My work, but with time they went away to make their life more comfortable because people bought them. So, when Satan sees a talented person, he brings different opportunities in their life, so that person may not reach his destiny, and he sells himself at a high price.

Many people whom I had selected in this city for My work if they were here today, this city would not have been like this. But seeing their qualities and abilities, they chose comfortable life and moved to a different place, despising My work. But the bad tomatoes [people], whom no one wanted, I am choosing such tomatoes now so that through them I can do My work in this city. When those I had chosen sold themselves for the facilities, luxuries and comforts of this world, those whom I did not choose, now I am choosing for a big cause.

Many of you who are sitting here today are rotten tomatoes. You are of no use in the eyes of this world. So, I am choosing people who will do an excellent job in this city. People whom nobody asks, who are only asked to clean tables and chairs, who are asked to broom and mop. Those who dream that I will also stand on the stage and sing a song one day.

I have started My work. More prayers are needed in the coming days because many are called, and very few have been chosen. Dedicate yourself. I want to use you. Will you allow me, asks the Lord God Almighty.

In His firm grip,

Evans Francis

Message from The Lord - 08-09-2022

While I was working, the Sovereign Lord asked me to tell you that you are valuable to Him. Nothing in this world can take your place. So, rejoice and be glad, for this is the will of God.

In His firm grip,

Evans Francis

Dream from The Lord – 14ᵗʰ September 2022

As I lay down to rest in the afternoon, the Sovereign Lord showed me a dream. In my dream, I saw a boy in school.

He was there in his classroom. Immediately a group of three boys came inside the classroom. These were fair and muscular boys. As they came inside, he ran to greet them, but one boy pushed him out of the way and said, "Out of my way." Then, as this boy was going back, another boy said, "You are so weak, you'll need me to satisfy your wife."

To those who are being bullied, know that God cares for you. I know it's hard, but know that God is your strength, ever present in trouble. Hold on to Him. Do not quit. Do not give up. Those who bully you today will come to you for help. Stay calm and focused, says the Lord God Almighty.

In His firm grip,

Evans Francis

Message from The Lord – 16ᵗʰ September 2022

While praying, a message from the Lord came to me saying, Son, as leaves grow on a tree but after its days, it automatically falls from the tree, likewise, every person born is appointed to die one day.

As leaves fall due to heavy wind and storms, when My people face heavy opposition in their life, they quit. Sometimes the leaves fall when an animal or bird plucks them out. The leaves die just like how the devil often comes and destroys My people's life prematurely.

Remember, I had chosen you before you were born, so when you go through tough times, know that I am with you. You are born with a purpose, don't allow the devil to destroy it, says the Lord God Almighty.

In His firm grip,

Evans Francis

Message from The Lord – 23ʳᵈ September 2022

While I was working, the Sovereign Lord said to me, as in the days of Noah, when water covered all the world, in the same way, before I return, there is going to be a heavy outpouring of the Holy Spirit in this world.

An outpouring greater than the first, and I will use ordinary people to do mighty works, and powerful miracles, as wonders, and signs will take place through them. I will use those who are awake, and those who are asleep will miss it, says the Lord God Almighty.

In His firm grip,

Evans Francis

Dream from The Lord – 11th October 2022

This morning the Sovereign Lord showed me a dream. In my dream, I saw an airport where people were preparing an aeroplane which was about to take off with passengers. But unfortunately, I saw a person who was very careless in his work, and as the plane took off from the runway, it started to burn from its tail, and ultimately, the aeroplane crashed. People of God, pray that such an incident should not take place. No premature deaths in Jesus' name.

In His firm grip,

Evans Francis

Message from The Lord – 1st November 2022

Today while working, by mistake my cell phone fell into the dustbin. Without thinking a second, I put my hand inside and started searching for it. While searching, my hands got dirty, but I got my cell phone back.

Unexpectedly, the Lord spoke to me. He said, "Son, in the same manner, My people should be ready to go into the dirt to win a soul. For a mobile phone worth a few thousand, without thinking you put your hand inside the dustbin. How much worth is a soul to Me?

Don't be afraid to get dirty while saving a soul from dirt, sinful situations," says the Lord God Almighty.

In His firm grip,

Evans Francis

Dream from the Lord – 12th November 2022

This morning the Sovereign Lord showed me a dream. In my dream, I saw the death of an older woman who did not accept Jesus as her Lord and Saviour.

In 16 years of ministry, I have never seen such a dream. It was scary and hellish. I saw an older woman who was lying on the floor. She must have been in her nineties. The Lord opened my spiritual eyes, and I could see the Spirit was leaving and coming back into her. At last, the Spirit left her, and I saw smoke coming out of her body, and I understood she was in hell. Something strange happened, she was dead, but she opened her eyes, and her eyes were not human but of an animal. When I saw her eyes, I felt in my Spirit, the devil saying, "I got her."

By the time you read this post, thousands have entered hell, and what have you done? Time to ponder.

In His firm grip,

Evans Francis

Dream from the Lord – 20th November 2022

This morning the Sovereign Lord showed me a couple of dreams. In my first dream, I saw many youngsters trying to catch a kite. It fell on another house's terrace. Everybody was giving their own advice. Finally, one boy went to the adjacent house and easily picked up the kite with his hands.

And the Lord said to me, "My people are going through problems because they listen to other people instead of My word. So, if they live according to My will, they will see My work taking place easily without any struggle."

In my second dream, I saw I had a small dove in my hand. I was holding this dove on the sixth or seventh floor of an apartment. Unexpectedly this dove flew and fell. Her wings were not strong enough to fly high.

I ran down the staircase, and as I came close to hold her again, she flew up, but this time without her knowledge, an eagle came and caught her. And the Lord made me feel what she felt. She thought I wish I had been in My master's hand. I would have been safe.

And the Lord said to me, those who remain in Me will be safe, but those who think they can do things on their own will become prey to the devil. So, my people need to learn to remain in My hands.

In His firm grip,

Evans Francis

Dream from the Lord – 24ᵗʰ November 2022

This morning the Sovereign Lord showed me a dream. In my dream, I saw somebody kidnap a person and lock him up in a room. Then, a person came, opened the door and said, "You are free to go." Firstly, this person could not believe and he went out rejoicingly.

And the Lord said to me that there are many whom the devil has kidnapped due to their negligence, but they will witness supernatural breakthroughs in their lives.

In His firm grip,

Evans Francis

Vision from The Lord – 30th November 2022

While working, the Sovereign Lord showed a school shooting taking place in the USA. So, people of God, pray against it. No premature deaths in Jesus' name.

In His firm grip,

Evans Francis

Message from The Lord – 9th December 2022

While I was praying, the Sovereign Lord said to me, if through one person Adam sin entered this mankind, and through one person - Jesus salvation came, know that one person is enough to change your entire life. Your destiny helper is on His way. So many have them but don't recognize them. On the contrary, they abuse them. Very few value them. One man with God is enough to strike down any situation. 1 Samuel 17:49

In His firm grip,

Evans Francis

Dream from The Lord – 16th December 2022

This morning the Sovereign Lord showed me a dream. In my dream, I saw two sparrows in a nest. There was food and water for them. They were enjoying themselves. Suddenly a massive sparrow came, thrice their size and started eating their food and pooping in their area. These small sparrows did nothing. After a few minutes, a big hand grabbed this giant sparrow and threw it in a cage.

And the Lord said to me that many of His children are not able to enjoy the blessings in their lives due to satan and the people used by him. Therefore, all My people need to do is stand still without taking matters into their own hands and wait upon Me. Days of Deliverance are ahead, says the Lord God Almighty.

In His firm grip,

Evans Francis

Dream from The Lord – 30th December 2022

As I lay down to rest this afternoon, the Sovereign Lord showed me a dream. In my dream, I saw a service going on in a church where approximately five hundred people were sitting. I saw two people sitting in the front row, claiming to be servants of God.

Next, I saw the pastor of that Church as he started to preach. The work of the Holy Spirit was very powerful as the Word of God was being preached. The pastor allowed the Holy Spirit to work and worshipped, closing his eyes. When the pastor opened his eyes, these two individuals who claimed to be servants of God were on stage and pushing people down on the ground. Humbly the pastor said, "Please go back to your place." When they went back to their seats, the pastor asked them who asked them to come on stage. This made these two individuals very upset, and they went out.

Next, I saw the pastor in his car with his wife, and suddenly, these two individuals started to attack his vehicle. The pastor drove his vehicle and escaped. Next, I saw he was in his house, and these two individuals came to his house and started attacking. There was fear in this pastor's family, and I woke up.

And the Lord said to me, these are My so-called servants, wolves in sheep's clothing, who claim to work for Me but are disgracing My name.

In His firm grip,

Evans Francis